TRANSPORTS OF DELIGHT
AN AROMATIC JOURNEY IN VERSE
FROM EAST TO WEST
ON THE WINGS OF PERFUME

Transports of Delight

AN AROMATIC JOURNEY IN VERSE
FROM EAST TO WEST
ON THE WINGS OF PERFUME

David Pybus

GLOBAL
ORIENTAL

TRANSPORTS OF DELIGHT
AN AROMATIC JOURNEY IN VERSE FROM
EAST TO WEST ON THE WINGS OF PERFUME

First published in 2007 by
GLOBAL ORIENTAL LTD
PO Box 219
Folkestone
Kent CT20 2WP
UK

www.globaloriental.co.uk

© David Pybus 2007

ISBN 978-1-905246-56-4

British Library Cataloguing in Publication Data
A CIP catalogue entry for this book is available
from the British Library

Set in Garamond by Mark Heslington, Scarborough, North Yorkshire
Printed and bound in England by Athenaeum Press, Gateshead, Tyne & Wear

Contents

Europe

Americas

Epilogue

Acknowledgements

As an Aromancer I like to try and get people to stop and smell the roses (or, indeed, the coffee!). This book was inspired by that thought, and supported from five different directions.

Praise must first be given to other people's flowers. To those men and women throughout history who have come out in verse and anecdote exalting perfumes and their impact on us. For it is they who have allowed me to gather this garden of flowers for you.

Thanks to the perfumers of Quest International, Ashford, Kent, which in March 2007 was absorbed into Givaudan to become part of the largest company of its kind involved in the human senses of smell and taste. Names like Roger Duprey, Mike Evans, Jorge Lee, Montserrat Moline, Chris Piddock, Chris Sheldrake and Les Small spring to mind as people who share my passion for this fabulous industry. I should also acknowledge the fact that my own creative urges have been encouraged by Linda Harman of Quest's publicity department, and also by Sergio Lievano, my true creative partner in many madcap inspirations.

I am grateful to those publishers who have responded giving permission to print where copyright was an issue, including Random House (*Memoirs of a Geisha*), and also to Bukkyō Dendō Kyōkai for the extract from The Teachings of Buddha.

Finally, thanks to Paul Norbury of Global Oriental, whose shared feelings for the sense of smell encouraged him to publish a book a little outside the normal orbit of his company.

As this book comes to market I can announce my success on the BBC2 TV programme 'Dragons' Den'. My desire to launch perfumes lost in time and 'resurrect' them, as it were, for today's effervescent market as 'Scents of Time' will come to fruition in late 2007 when Cleopatra's perfume, Sperato of Pompeii's unguent and Jehovah's designer fragrance will finally see the light of day.

The publishers and I have made every effort to contact authors/copyright holders of works reprinted in *Transports of Delight*. This has not been possible in every case, however, and we would welcome correspondence from those individuals and companies we have been unable to trace.

From The Ballad of East and West

RUDYARD KIPLING (1865–1936)

Oh, East is East, and West is West, and
never the twain shall meet,
Till Earth and Sky stand presently
at God's great Judgment Seat;
But there is neither East nor West, Border,
nor Breed, nor Birth,
When two strong men stand face to face, tho'
they come from the ends of the earth!

Prologue

As I sit in my study completing this anthology, the smoke of incense drifts across the room, and I am instantly transported to the other side of our planet. To a land of Buddhist temples and Shinto shrines. To the fabled Orient of aromatic wonders.

It is not at all difficult for me, therefore, to appreciate how proximate and related our sense of smell is, deep within our brain in the limbic system, to our seat of memory. The 'rhinocephalon' or smell-brain, is the most ancient part of our human sensory make-up. Wrapped around it are all the layers of grey matter that eventually developed our species into homo sapiens.

Formed when our ancestors were literally in the primordial soup, the primitive smell-brain was all they needed to both smell and taste food in the deep oceans of our early beginnings. Connected, too, with the instinctive 'fight or flight' mechanism of our beings, and to the elaborate mechanism of our sexual gonads, small wonder that sex, smell and soul are integrally linked.

All of which goes part way to explaining why aromas are true 'transports of delight' for humans, and how they are able to mix and match our moods, enhance our emotions, provoke a sense of awe in the natural world around us, tantalize our travels, bring us closer to our gods, promote our passions and revive our romances.

Which brings me to this book. I have always been fascinated with our sense of smell, not only because it is a God-given sense which allows us to appreciate the good things in life, but because it has also given me a career of over thirty years in the cosmetic, toiletry and perfumery business. As a perfume historian I have been privileged to take more account of, and get more stimulation from, our oldest, and probably our most complex, sense. One that the majority of us take entirely for granted, but one that, because of its deep-seated place in our make-up, can at the same time provoke profound sensations in all of us.

In the ancient scripts of India our senses were likened to the five horses of a chariot – unruly and highly charged. Diverting, given rein, to all the compass directions. To progress, and move forward the chariot of our mind, they needed to be reined in, calmed and made to work in concert with one another.

There are three pathways in life. The left-hand way is the hedonistic way. The way of the senses. One in which all olfactory, visual, auditory, touch and taste sensations are explored and enjoyed to the full. Where our chemical beings are sounded by the vibrations of photic, electric, sonic and magnetic energies and respond in full to them. The right-hand path is one of meditation and reflection. That of stilling the mind, quelling the senses and finding our true existence in cosmic consciousness, outside of the illusions of Maya which surround us.

For many, the short-term left-hand path is the easiest. 'There are no rehearsals for life' is their credo. Others, perhaps religion-inspired, manage the harder right-hand path in the full belief that this particular life is one of many on the road to complete enlightenment.

For the moment, I walk the middle way, probably with the majority, diverting from time to time to indulge the senses, whilst at other times seeking consolation by reflection, prayer and both physical and mental practices such as Tai Chi and Yoga.

Nothing is new under the sun, and as I began to indulge my interest in the sense of smell, I quickly realized that many had gone before me with that same interest and acknowledgement, and that whatever our creed, culture or colour, common ground was to be found in our appreciation of aromas, and the manner in which they switched us on. And that this appreciation manifests itself in a number of ways.

In our sensory world of smell, East and West truly do meet.

Through incense we prayed to our gods and found transcendental states. Through aromatics we developed trade routes, which spanned the known world, bringing two strong men face to face in barter. Bringing the Orient to the Occident and vice versa.

Through perfume we find romance, and indulge in passion. Through travel we collect olfactive memories and sensations of different countries and climes. Through people we discover the joys of togetherness, and sometimes the pitfalls of enticement and allure. Through our deep-seated love of nature we share a common bond which will hopefully mean that in the longer term our planet is truly preserved for generations to come, and that our special relationship with it, lost in the frenetic adrenal rush of the industrial and information ages, is rekindled again for the good of all.

The Ballad of East and West is set in Afghanistan. Known

as the crossroads of Asia, Afghanistan is surrounded by mountainous terrain, which was crossed only by those traders intrepid enough to risk life and limb in the pursuit of profit, carrying as they did by camel and horse those most valuable of materials – invariably light in weight but highly desirable the more distance travelled. And in some cases the journeys were measured in years.

There were a number of major staging posts on the Silk Road and Incense Trail which linked Asia with Europe. At one end stood Nara, ancient capital of Japan, across the sea from fabled Xanadu, seat of the Mongol Emperors of China, the next major land stage. A thousand miles inland from Xanadu are the borders of the Taklamakan desert, whose Uyghur name means 'he who goes in does not come out'. This desert of terror stretches for six hundred hard-won miles, and boasts dunes of up to a thousand feet high. At one end stood the Jade Gate, entrance to China proper, whilst Kashgar at the far end, marked the ultimate borders of the Chinese Empire.

Whilst nowadays this desert is a major challenge to cross, three thousand years ago receding glaciers in the Himalayan foothills had created lush oases at intervals along the way which in this otherwise waterless waste meant the difference between life and death. From Kashgar, crossing over the high mountain ranges of the Karakoram and Hindu Kush, Kabul in Afghanistan stood at the trade junction of Asia with the Indian sub-continent and Europe. Here Khitan, Mongol and Uyghur met Arab, African, Indian and European eager for trade.

From thence silk and incense materials found their way to Constantinople, Venice, Jerusalem, Alexandria, the Moghul cities of India and the far-flung corners of Western Europe, including the British Isles. And this trade in precious commodities was of course two-way.

Buddhism took incense east from India and Tibet through China to Japan. Judaism and Christianity took frankincense west from Jerusalem to all the lands of the Holy Roman Empire. Islam took aromatics through the Arabian peninsula into Africa and the East Indies. In northern Spain and southern France the Arab legacy of raw materials and chemical methods led to a sophisticated perfume industry that exists in Western Europe today. For the Arabs not only developed natural aromas, but also the elixir alcohol to trap them in. The final link in this journey took place hundreds of years later, when the Pilgrim Fathers crossed the Atlantic Ocean in a vessel appropriately named Mayflower, taking with them man's legacy of aromatic appreciation, and learning much in addition from the Amerindians they met in the new lands. Wagon trains moved westwards across the buffalo-strewn prairies and through the passes of the Rockies, soon to be followed by the 'Iron Horse' railway. All of which allows this anthology to travel the perfumed path of our planet from Japan westwards to link the whole world.

Living as I do in Kent, on the south coast of England, I am aware of its strong links to this global pathway. For it is here that the crusaders landed after their Holy Wars, bringing the scented distillations of Arabia to the cold, dank castles of England. From that moment on, spices from around the world arrived in abundance at Dover, and a few centuries later from the West at Bristol. And it is here, in Folkestone, that Sir William Harvey, famed as one of the fathers of modern medicine because of his work on the circulation of the blood, gained his expensive education supported by the family wealth based on the silk trade along that same well-trodden route.

In a sense I am using the Harvey heraldic crest (see back of book) as my leitmotif for this work. (Their motto, *Arde Piv, Piv Splende*, means 'more effort, more reward'.) In four symbols it shows, to my mind both the jagged mountains and billowing seas, representing the physical hardships of travel along the Silk Road and Incense Trail, with the distorted Templar Cross of Christianity and Moorish Crescent of Islam illustrating the bond in trade and fellowship between two of the world's great religions.

□

And so to the poems themselves. Over the last twenty years or so I have collected a 'Book of Smells', which is a compilation of anecdotes, poetry and writings to do with our sense of smell, both good and bad.

Transports of Delight is a distillation of that work, where I have taken some of the greatest poets and most sensual writers of our times and spiced them at intervals with my own offerings to the gods, ensuring the twenty-four-thousand-mile journey across our planet by sea and land is completely linked, and fairly representative.

Passion and romance are explored in a variety of ways, from the gentle verses of Genji, Michizane and Sen Rikyu to the more sensuous renderings of Robert Herrick and Edmund Spenser.

Memory is recalled by the various works of Symons and Johnson, striking a note also in the renderings of the *Kokinshū*.

Our love of nature is echoed in the works of Li Kuang-

T'ien, Chief Seathl, Walt Whitman and Vachel Lindsay amongst others.

Perfume, as such, is exalted in the writings of Wratislaw, Baudelaire, Keats and Matsuo Basho.

Conrad, Polo and Kipling expound the joys and mysteries of travel, and Divan of Hafiz its hardships, whilst the stories of Herodotus well illustrate to what lengths the traders of incense materials went in the protection of their sources.

Allure and enticement are exemplified by the works of Arthur Godden, Sir Edwin Arnold, Francis Faulkes and Ralph Knevet. An Edict by George III shows to what extent the tools of entrapment were regarded as criminal by Georgian England.

Perfume is derived from 'per fumum', the Latin for 'by' or 'through smoke'. For it was in this way, by the smoke of incense, that the words of our prayers were sweetened in their passage beyond the invisible barrier between Earth and Heaven. Religion and incense are treated by, amongst others, The Way of Practical Attainment, 10 Uses of Koh and the prayers of many along the incense trail. The Bible, too, has much to say on the subject, from the steamy lover's rendering in the Song of Songs to Jehovah's own designer recipe.

Finally, man's search for the elixir of youth is promulgated by The Ordinall of Alchemy and Secret of the Philosophers. In medieval times people believed that the quintessence, or distillation of being, was created from the four elements of earth, water, air and fire. How clearly this is the case with flowers, nature's own perfume factories. Their roots seek the Earth, whence they take up Water and nutrients. They draw in Air, and, by photosynthesis, employing the Fiery light of the sun, they manufacture their aromatic allure for all to appreciate in their quest to procreate by pollination.

The puffers' quest was aided by a mixture of work, labour and prayer, in a small oratory designed for the purpose. From this alchemical practice our modern laboratories of science were derived. For in the search to improve our lives, and have experimental success, dialogue with our gods is still a necessary process.

All in all, I hope I have prepared a pot-pourri to delight the senses and provide a feast for the nose.

DAVID PYBUS
Sandgate, Folkestone
February 2007

Scent

DAVID PYBUS (1947–)

Scent, perfume, fragrance,
Bouquet, incense, spicery,
Tutti frutti, flower power
Or just plain 'smelly'?

Bottled figment, phialled elixir,
Holy smoke and stuff of dreams,
Break the seal, remove the stopper,
Loose the gaseous Djinni's streams.

Mottled myrrh from Araby,
Crinkled clove of Zanzibar,
Speckled spice of Samarkand,
Wrinkled weed from Malabar.

Wood and fruit and fragrant bloom,
Burst forth from their crystal tomb,
Swarms of smell spill out pell-mell
To wrap you into their sweet womb.

Balmy nights and dreamy days,
Mountain streams and tropic shore,
Balsams, resins, wisps and sprays,
Odours gathered by the score.

Sensual smokes, aroused aromas,
Gifts from gods and joy of man,
Love's explosives in small doses,
Reach Nirvana if you can.

JAPAN

Fragrance of the Orange

KOKINSHŪ III: 139 (JAPAN, EARLY 10TH CENTURY)

ANON

Satsuki matsu
Hanatachibana no
Ka o kageba
Mukashi no hito no
Sode no ka zo suru

Fragrance of the orange,
Flowering at last in June,
Wafts through the summer night
The memory of scented sleeves
Of someone long ago.

Once there was a Man

THE TEACHINGS OF BUDDHA – 13
The Way of Practical Attainment
From BUKKYŌ DENDŌ KYŌKAI

Once there was a man burning incense.
He noticed that the fragrance
Was neither coming nor going:
It neither appeared nor disappeared.
This trifling incident
Led him to enlightenment.

10 Uses of Koh (Incense)

16TH CENTURY, JAPAN

Koh aids transcendental meditation
Koh purifies both mind and body
Koh removes uncleanliness
Koh keeps you alert
Koh provides a companion in the midst of solitude.

Koh brings tranquility in a busy world
Plentiful use of Koh never tires
Sparing use of Koh always satisfies
Age does not change Koh's potency
Everyday use of Koh is not harmful.

Brought by the Breeze

TEA-MASTER SHUNZAI'S DAUGHTER
KOKINSHŪ (JAPAN, EARLY 10TH CENTURY)

Brought by the breeze,
The scent of flowers in my sleeve
Is what awakens me
On a pillow richly fragrant
With the brief spring night of dreams.

An Ephemeral Spring Dream

KOKINSHŪ (JAPAN, EARLY 10TH CENTURY)

An ephemeral spring dream –
The plum's colour
Is lost in the night
Would it be possible
To hide the fragrance?

In the Moonlight

KOKINSHŪ (JAPAN, EARLY 10TH CENTURY)

In the moonlight
Where are the plum blossoms?
Let their fragrance guide you.
The fragrance –
More alluring than the colour –
Whose scented sleeves have brushed
The blossoms in my garden?

Flowers of Hill or Dale

SEN RIKYU (1522–91)

Flowers of hill or dale
Put them in a simple vase
Full or brimming o'er
But when you're arranging them
You must slip your heart in too.

When the East Wind Blows

SUGAWARA MICHIZANE (845–903)

When the east wind blows,
Send me your perfume,
Blossoms of the plum:
Though your Lord be absent
Forget not the spring.

After Bells had Rung

MATSUO BASHO (1644–94)

After bells had rung
And were silent...
Flowers chimed
A peal of fragrance.
What bloom on what tree
Yields
This imperceptible
Essence of incense?

From Memoirs of a Geisha

ARTHUR GOLDEN (1956–)

In Gion, Mahema said, a very popular geisha can always make sure her younger sister earns more than anyone else – if she is willing to risk hurting her own reputation. The reason has to do with the way ohana, 'flower fees', are billed. In the old days, a hundred years or more ago, every time a geisha arrived at a party to entertain, the mistress of the tea-house lit a stick of one-hour incense – called one ohana, or 'flower'. The geisha's fees were based on how many sticks of incense had burned by the time she left.

The cost of one ohana has always been fixed by the Gion Registry Office. While I was an apprentice, it was Y3, which is about the cost of two bottles of liquor, perhaps. It may sound like a lot, but an unpopular geisha earning one ohana per hour had a grim life. Probably she spends most evenings sitting around the charcoal brazier waiting for an engagement; even when she's busy she may earn no more than Y10 a night, which won't be enough even to pay back her debts. Considering all the wealth that would flow into Gion, she's nothing more than an

22

insect picking at a carcass – compared to Hatsumamo or Mahema, who are magnificent lionesses feasting at the kill, not only because they have engagements all night long every night, but because they charge one ohana every fifteen minutes, rather than one every hour, and in the case of Mahema ... well, there as no one else in Gion quite like her; she charged one ohana every five minutes.

From The Musmee

SIR EDWIN ARNOLD (1832–1904)

The Musmee wears a wondrous dress —
Kimono, obi, imoji —
A rose-bush in Spring-loveliness
Is not more colour-glad to see!
Her girdle holds her silver pipe,
And heavy swing her long silk sleeves
With cakes, love-letters, *mikan* ripe,
Small change, musk-box and writing-leaves.

From The Buddha at Kamakura

RUDYARD KIPLING (1865–1936)

O ye who tread the Narrow Way
By Tophet-flare to Judgement Day,
Be gentle when 'the heathen' pray
To Buddha at Kamakura!

To him the Way, the Law, apart,
Whom Maya held beneath her heart,
Ananda's Lord, the Bodhisat,
The Buddha of Kamakura.

For though he neither burns nor sees,
Nor hears ye thank your Dieties,
Ye have not sinned with such as these,
His children at Kamakura,

Yet spare us still the Western joke
When joss sticks turn to scented smoke
The little sins of little folk
That worship at Kamakura –

The grey-robed, gay-sashed butterflies
That flit beneath the Master's eyes.
He is beyond the Mysteries
But loves them at Kamakura.

CHINA, TIBET
AND
EAST INDIES

When Two People are at One

I CHING (ca. 825 BC)

When two people are at one in their
innermost hearts,
They shatter even the strength
of iron or bronze,
– and when
two people understand each other
in their innermost hearts,
Their words are sweet and strong
like the fragrance of orchids.

Xanadu

From KUBLA KHAN
OR, A VISION IN A DREAM
SAMUEL TAYLOR COLERIDGE (1772–1834)

In Xanadu did Kubla Khan
A stately pleasure-dome decree:
Where Alph, the sacred river, ran
Through caverns measureless to man
Down to a sunless sea.
So twice five miles of fertile ground
With walls and towers were girdled round:
And there were gardens bright with sinuous rills,
Where blossom'd many an incense-bearing tree:
And here were forests ancient as the hills,
Enfolding sunny spots of greenery.

The Glories of Kinsay (Hangchow)

From 'THE MEDIEVAL SOURCEBOOK'
MARCO POLO (1254–1324)

All the ten market places are encompassed by lofty houses, and below these are shops where all sorts of crafts are carried on, and all sorts of wares are on sale, including spices and jewels and pearls. Some of these shops are entirely devoted to the sale of wine made from rice and spices, which is constantly made fresh, and is sold very cheap.

Certain of the streets are occupied by the women of the town, who are in such number that I dare not say what it is. They are found not only in the vicinity of the marketplaces, where usually a quarter is assigned to them, but all over the city. They exhibit themselves splendidly attired and abundantly perfumed, in finely garnished houses, with trains of waiting-women.

These women are extremely accomplished in all the arts of allurement, and readily adapt their conversation to all sorts of persons, insomuch that strangers who have once tasted their attractions seem to get bewitched, and are so taken with their blandishments and their fascinating ways that they never can get these out of their heads. Hence it comes to pass that when they return home they say they have been to Kinsay or the City of Heaven, and their only desire is to get back thither as soon as possible.

Compiler's note:
In his travels Marco Polo made much mention of aromatic materials and their sources. Musk from Tibet, aloes from Vietnam and Laos, cassia in China, clove, sandalwood and ambergris from the islands of the Indian Ocean and East Indian Archipelago.

The Scent of Autumn

LI KUANG-T'IEN

TRANSLATED FROM THE CHINESE BY KAI-YUTTSU

Who has smelled the scent of Autumn
While looking at a garden from a window with tattered
curtains?
From distant lakes
The scent of rotten leaves fallen on the marshes,
And from the depth of a forest
The smell of ripe berries on withered branches
Are brought here by a good breeze.
The scent of Autumn?
The scent
Wakes me up from an old dream,
So faint,
Like the autumn clouds this moment
Being blown along by the western wind,
And again blown away,
As I gaze at them from the window.

Hymn to Incense

TAOIST LITURGY

Official Envoys of the incense, Lords of the
Dragon and Tiger to the left and right, Golden
Girls and Boys attending upon the fragrance,
and all Divine Beings cause that at this place
where I have today conducted an audience, the
divine mushroom of immortality, cinnabar and
jade green, may spontaneously grow out of the
golden liquor, and that the host of Perfected
Immortals may meet in unity at this ardent
incense burner.

May the Immortal Youths and Jade Girls of the
ten directions smile upon and protect this
incense, and transfer swiftly all that I have said
before the heavenly throne of the Supremely
Honoured Jade Emperor.

The Widow's Tale

AH-LONG (888–947)
PRAYER OF A 64-YEAR-OLD DUNHUANG
(CHINA SILK-ROAD) WOMAN
(ca. TENTH CENTURY)

I offer this incense to announce the misfortunes
that rain
Down upon me as fast as the lightning sent by
the god
Luling. I beg that my prayers will reach the ears
of the Star
God Rahu, and that he will force the hundred
demons that
Beset me to go far away, that he will strengthen
the power of the good spirits,
Let my illnesses fade away day after day, year after
year.
I entreat him for happiness and blessing, for the
End of my misfortunes and to pardon my sins.

From Lord Jim

JOSEPH CONRAD (1857–1924)

The hospital stood on a hill, and a gentle breeze entering through the windows, always flung wider open, brought into the bare room the softness of the sky, the languor of the earth, the bewitching breath of Eastern waters. There were perfumes in it, suggestions of infinite repose, the gift of endless dreams.

Burning Incense

LAMA ANAGARIKA GOVINDA (1898–1985)

A gentle column of frankincense is rising;
Transparently shimmering like crystal,
Airy blue like the distant horizon,
Vibrating like a note played on a violin.

A gentle veil descends from the dark ceiling,
Into the quiet space:
Toning the warm glow of the candle,
Cooling the glowing colour of the flowers,
Shrouding the golden head of the Buddha
In the distance.

But three monks sitting, immersed in thought,
In the late hour stillness of the room:
They never see the splendour of the flowers,
They do not hear the crackle of the candle's flame,
No more can they feel the beat of the heart.

Buddha's golden countenance itself
Is erased from their soul:
They only see the column of frankincense,
They only sense the crystal-like clarity,
They only hear the vibrating sound,
Imagining the faraway horizon.

INDIA
AND
THE LEVANT

Soft as a Bud

SANSKRIT POEM

Soft as a bud her betel-scarlet lips
Skin stained with sandal paste, and brimming eyes
Running eye shadow as the fountain sprays;
Damp hair, flower-scented, dripping dress that grips
And shows her body all – what charms arise
From beauty bathing late on summer days!

When We Have Loved

FROM THE SANSKRIT
TRANSLATION BY JOHN BROUGH (1917–84)

When we have loved, my love,
Panting and pale from love,
Then from your cheeks, my love,
Scent of the sweat I love;
And when our bodies love
Now to relax in love,
After the stress of love,
Ever still more I love
Our mingled breath of love.

In the Month of Vaishaka*

From THE BARAMASA, A SET OF TWELVE LOVE POEMS
SET IN THE MONTHS OF THE YEAR.
KESHAVA DASA (LATE-SIXTEENTH CENTURY)

The earth and sky
are filled with fragrance:
a gentle, sweet-smelling
breeze blows softly.

Beauty is everywhere
and perfume
pervades the air,
inebriating the bee
and filling with longing
the heart of the lover
far from home.

I beseech you,
who have made me
so happy,
not to leave me
in the month of Vaishaka.

The arrows
of the love-god Kama
are difficult to bear
during separation.

* Springtime – April/May

The Prophet

KAHLIL GIBRAN (1883–1931)

And a merchant said: 'Speak to us of Buying and Selling.'

And he answered and said:

'To you the earth yields her fruit, and you shall not want if you but know how to fill your hands.

It is in exchanging the gifts of the earth that you shall find abundance and be satisfied.

Yet unless the exchange be in love and kindly justice, it will but lead some to greed and others to hunger.

When in the market-place you toilers of the sea and fields and vineyards meet the weavers and the potters and the gatherers of spices, –

Invoke then the master spirit of the earth, to come into your midst and sanctify the scales and the reckoning that weighs value against value.

And suffer not the barren-handed to take part in your transactions, who would sell their words for your labour.'

To such men you should say:

'Come with us to the field, or go with our brothers to the sea and cast your net;

For the land and the sea shall be bountiful to you even as to us.'

And if there come the singers and the dancers and the flute players, – buy of their gifts also.

For they too are gatherers of fruit and frankincense, and that which they bring, though fashioned of dreams, is raiment and food for your soul.

And before you leave the market-place, see that no one has gone his way with empty hands.

For the master spirit of the earth shall not sleep peacefully upon the wind till the needs of the least of you are satisfied.

Awake, O Heart

DIVAN OF HAFIZ (1310–88)

Awake, O Heart, an early breeze
Is softly sighing in the trees;
A swift-winged Nightingale has brought
Me Myrrh and Spices from the South
And Rumours of the wonders seen
Within the courts of Sheba's Queen,
Where amorous breezes gently stir
Above the languid head of her
Whose image still tormenteth me
Across the golden foaming sea.

Song of Arabian Camel Drovers

(At the start of their trail in Ethiopia and Somalia)

ANON

O, men of the caravan!
We have loaded the camels.
Now we make our way across the desolate plain
Where spirits fly
And vultures and hyenas hold orgies on the dead.

O, men of the caravan!
Ever since our eyes saw the sun
Have we roamed the desolate plain
Where Death lurks
And Djinns screech in the thorn bushes.

O, men of the caravan!
If enemies cross our path,
Then pursue them and spit them on your spears,
And when they have fled
The poorest lad among you will be a man of gold.

O, men of the caravan!
Wipe your sweat-covered brows.
See in a vision the purple-coloured shadow
Where the air is cool
And flower-clad maidens dance in a scent of myrrh.

O, camels,
Come my camels.
Can you smell the nearness of the water?
Can you catch the fragrance of the desert rose?
May Allah protect us from all robbers.

The Capture of a Rose by Distillation

EDWARD POWYS MATHERS (1892–1939)

My visit is shorter than a ghost's
between winter it is, and summer.
Hasten to play with me, play with me;
Time is a sword.

I wear my beauty in a crystal shift of dew.
Men hurry me from my green to another crystal;
My body turns to water, my heart is burned,
My tears are collected
And my flesh is torn.
I feel the passion of fire,
My flesh is fumed off,
My spirit goes in vapour,
The passionate
Breathe the Musk of my cast garments with delight;
My body goes from you, but my soul remains.

From The Rubaiyat of Omar Khayyam

OMAR KHAYYAM (1048–1122)

TRANSLATION, EDWARD FITZGERALD (1809–83)

I sometimes think that never blows so red
The rose as where some buried Caesar bled
That every hyacinth the garden wears
Dropt in its lap from some once lovely head ...

... Ah, with the grape my failing life provide
And wash my body whence the life has died
And in the winding sheet of vine leaf wrapt,
So bury me by some sweet garden side.

That ev'n my buried ashes such a snare
Of perfume shall fling up into the air
As not a true believer passing by
But shall be overtaken unaware.

And when thyself with shining foot shall pass
Among the guests star-scatter'd on the grass
And in thy joyous errand reach the spot
Where I made one – turn down an empty glass.

Gulistan (Garden of a Rose)

SADI (1207?–1291)

A sweet-smelling piece of clay, one day in the bath
Came from the hand of a beloved one to my hand.
I asked: 'Art thou musk or ambergris?
Because thy delicious odour intoxicates me.'
It replied, 'I was a despicable lump of clay;
But for a while in the society of a rose.
The perfection of my companion took effect on me,
And if not, I am the same earth which I am!'

Sinbad's Other Tale

DAVID PYBUS (1947–)

The Sperm it feeds on cuttlefish,
By all accounts a tasty dish
But not the bones that stomach cut
And form great scars upon the gut.

Which when the whale has had enough
And promptly sickens of the stuff
Ejects this morass on the sea,
Where 'mermaid's gold' awaits for me.

As Allah's gift is worked upon,
By wind and waves, by rain and sun,
To give aromas of delight
Which sets the nose of man alight
And this I sell for princely sum
In Basra's market, where all come.

Alas, I cannot tell this tale,
Of Ambergris which comes from whale.
I need protect my trade you see,
And thus a story tell to thee.

Of abyss-edge, where fiery pits
Throw out the ambergris in bits,
So only bold will venture forth
And sail to East, West, South and North.

For with such dangers on the sea
Much safer 'tis to buy from me,
And rest assured they all come back
For nature's aphrodisiac.

I praise Allah for this bounty,
So wondrous made upon the sea.

Incantation

TOMB OF AHMOSE

PHARAONIC EGYPT

Take to thee Lotus flowers and plants and
Lotus buds when they recur as every bloom
and every herb of sweet odour at its season;
cool water and incense, joints and offering
requirement in full tale, that thy Ka may be
satisfied with them for ever and ever.

Take Unto Thee Sweet Spices

HOLY BIBLE: EXODUS 30 (KING JAMES VERSION)

34   And the Lord said unto Moses, Take unto thee sweet spices, stacte and onycha and galbanum; *these* sweet spices with frankincense; of each there shall be a like *weight*:

35   And thou shalt make of it a perfume, a confection after the art of the apothecary, tempered together, pure and holy:

36   And thou shalt beat *some* of it very small, and put of it before the testimony in the tabernacle of the congregation, where I will meet with thee; it shall be unto you most holy.

37   And *as for* the perfume which thou shalt make, ye shall not make to yourselves according to the composition thereof: it shall be unto thee holy for the Lord.

38   Whosoever shall make like unto that, to smell thereto, shall even be cut off from his people.

The Smell of Lebanon

HOLY BIBLE: SONG OF SONGS, CHAPTER 4 (KING JAMES VERSION)

11   Thy lips, O *my* spouse, drop *as* the honeycomb:
      honey and milk *are* under thy tongue;
      and the smell of thy garments
      is like the smell of Lebanon.

12   A garden enclosed *is* my sister, *my* spouse;
         a spring shut up, a fountain sealed.

13   Thy plants *are* an orchard of pomegranates,
         with pleasant fruits; camphire and spikenard,

14   Spikenard and saffron; calamus and cinnamon,
         with all the trees of frankincense;
            myrrh and aloes,
         with all the chief spices:

15   A fountain of gardens,
            a well of living waters,
         and streams from Lebanon.

16   Awake, O north wind; and come thou south;
         Blow upon my garden,
      that the spices thereof may flow out.
      Let my beloved come into his garden,
         And eat his pleasant fruits.

From The Gardener

RABINDRANATH TAGORE (1861–1941)

Who are you, reader, reading my poems an
hundred years hence?
I cannot send you one single flower from this
wealth of the spring, one single streak of gold
from yonder clouds.
Open your doors and look abroad.
From your blossoming garden gather fragrant
memories of the vanished flowers of a hundred
years before.
In the joy of your heart may you feel the living
joy that sang one spring morning, sending its
glad voice across an hundred years.

EUROPE

Here First She Bathes

HOMER (8TH CENTURY BC)

Here first she bathes and round her body pours
Soft oils of fragrance and ambrosial showers,
The winds perfumed, the balmy gale conveys
Through heaven and earth, and all her aerial ways.

When I Drink Wine

ANACREON (ca.572–488 BC)

When I drink wine my bliss is complete
Having bathed my body with ointment sweet,
And holding fast a maid in my arms,
I sing of the Cyprians' matchless charms.

The Histories

HERODOTUS (ca.484BC–ca.420BC)

(TRANSLATION, AUBREY DE SELINCOURT (1896–1962))

Again, the most southerly country is Arabia; and Arabia is the only place that produces frankincense, myrrh, cassia, cinnamon and the gum called ledanon. All these, except myrrh, cause the Arabians a lot of trouble to collect. When they gather frankincense, they burn storax (the gum which is brought into Greece by the Phoenicians) in order to raise a smoke to drive off the flying snakes; these snakes, the same which attempt to invade Egypt, are small in size and of various colours, and great numbers of them keep guard over the trees which bear the frankincense, and the only way to get rid of them is by smoking them out with storax …

… When the Arabians go out to collect cassia, they cover their bodies and faces, all but their eyes, with ox-hides and other skins. The plant grows in a shallow lake, which, together with the ground about it, is infested by winged creatures very like bats, which screech alarmingly and are very pugnacious. They have to be kept from attacking the men's eyes while they are cutting the cassia …

... The process of collecting cinnamon is still more remarkable. Where it comes from, and what country produces it, they do not know; the best some of them can do is to make a fair guess that it grows somewhere in the region that Dionysus was brought up. What they say is that the dry sticks, which we have learned from the Phoenicians to call cinnamon, are brought by large birds, which carry them to their nests, made of mud, on mountain precipices, which no man can climb, and that the method the Arabians have invented for getting hold of them is to cut up the bodies of dead oxen, or donkeys, or other animals into large joints, which they carry to the spot in question and leave on the ground near the nests. Then they retire to a safe distance, and the birds fly down and carry off the joints of meat to their nests, which not being strong enough to bear the weight, break and fall to the ground. Then the men come along and pick up the cinnamon, which is subsequently exported to other countries...

Still more surprising is the way of get ladanon – or ladanon, as the Arabians call it. Sweet-smelling substance though it is, it is found in a most malodorous place; sticking, namely, like glue in the beards of he-goats who have been browsing in the bushes. It is used as an ingredient in many kinds of perfume, and is what the Arabians chiefly burn as incense. So much for perfumes: let me only add that the whole country exhales a more than earthly fragrance.

Phoenix

OVID (43BC–17AD)

TRANSLATION, JOHN DRYDEN (1631–1700)

All these receive their birth from other things:
But from the Phoenix only springs
Self-born, begotten by the parent flame
In which he burn'd; another and the same;
... He (his five centuries of life eclare'd)
His nest on oaken boughs begins to build,
Or trembling tops of palm;..
Of cassia, cinnamon and stems of nard,
... till ethereal flame
First catches then consumes, this costly frame;
Consumes him too, as on the pile he lies:
He lives on odours, and in odours dies.
An infant Phoenix from the former springs,
His father's heir...
And the same lease of life on the same terms renews.

You Will Dine Well, Dear Fabullus

GAIUS VALERIUS CATTALUS (ca.84–ca.54BC)

You will dine well, dear Fabullus, at my place
In a few days, if the gods are kind to you,
If you bring along with you a dinner large,
And splendid, and yes, a charming girl as well,
And wine and wit and every kind of laughter.

If, as I say, you bring along these things, sweet friend,
You will dine well. For your Catallus' wallet
Is full of dust and cobwebs. But in return
You will receive the purest essence of love
Or something still more fragrant and more graceful,
For I'll provide a perfume which was given
To my girl by the Venuses and Cupids.

My Boy's Kisses

MARCUS VALERIUS MARTIALIS (ca.40–ca.102AD)

Breath of balm from phials of yesterday, of the last
effluence that falls from a curving jet of saffron; perfume
of apples ripening in their winter-chest, of fields lavish
with the leafage of spring; of Augusta's silken roses from
Palatine presses, of amber warmed by a maiden's hand, of
a garden that stays therein Sicilian bees; the scent of
Cosmus' alabaster boxes, and of the altars of the gods; of a
chaplet fallen but now from a rich man's locks – why
should I speak of these? Not enough are they; mix them
all; such is the fragrance of my boy's kisses at morn.

Poetry is Hard

APOLLINARIS SIDONIUS (AD 430–485)

Ah, poetry is hard, cast as I am amongst
Hairy hordes, deafened by the strife of the German tongue
Forced to laud the songs of a noisy Burgundian
With rancid fat in his hair, when all I feel is disgust.
Happy thine eyes, happy thine ears,
And even thy nose ...... for it is not forced
To sniff the stench of garlic or
Onions ten times each morn.

The Smell of Gum

ARNOBIUS (4TH CENTURY AD)

What is this sign of respect which comes
From the smell of gum of a tree burning in a fire?
Does this then, do you suppose,
Give honour to the heavenly magnates?
Or if their displeasure has been aroused at any time,
Is it really soothed and dissipated by incense's smoke?

But if it is smoke the gods want, why must it only be
incense?
If you answer that incense has a nice smell,
While other substances have not,
Tell me if the gods have nostrils to smell them?
But if the gods are incorporeal, odours and perfumes
Can have no effect at all upon them,
Since corporeal substances cannot affect incorporeal
beings.

Chypre (Cyprus)

DAVID PYBUS (1947–)

Cyprus casts a sorcerous smell,
That binds all in enchanted spell.
The magic scent that strikes a chord,
Is alchemy from nature's hoard
Of choice aromas, and the key
Is struck by heady mix of three.

The first springs from Hesperides
As bergamot sends charms from trees.
This mingles well with woody scent
Of mosses from the oak trees lent.
And both combine with labdanum,
A substance from the rock-rose won.

All three notes play in harmony
To pluck the heart-strings pleasantly
They homage pay to Chypre's isle.
Bewitching strangers all the while,
As Aphrodite's incense smoke
All human passions does invoke.

The Ordinall Of Alchemy

From 'THE ORDINALL OF ALCHEMY' (1447)
THOMAS NORTON (1532–84)

Old Fathers wrote by their doctrine,
Of their experience which is maturine,
That if ye medle sweete savour and redolente
Equally with stinking to prove your intent;
The soote shall be smelled, the stinking not soe,
The cause ye may lerne now ere ye goe;
All sweet smelling things have more puritie,
And are more spirituall than stinking maie be.
Pleasant odours ingendered shall be
Of clean and pure substance and fumigale;
As it appeareth in Amber, Narde and Mirrhe,
Good for a woman, such things pleaseth her;
But of pure substance with a Meane heate,
Be temperate odours as in Violet;
Of a Meane heate with substance impure,
Is odours misliking, as aloes and sulphure.

Secret of the Philosophers

DAVID PYBUS (1947–)

The Alchemist from days of yore
Employed the use of athanor
To aid the make of Gold go well,
And burnished bright his aludel.
These Puffers used glass alembics
To practise many kinds of tricks,
Distilling with a Bain-Marie
The roots and saps and balms of tree.

And caught the drops with a retort
So finely in the furnace wrought.
Whilst incense burned and prayer wheels span,
The amber liquid seethed and ran.
For charged he well his Pelikan
Whose beak exudes the quest of man,
Strange mixtures bubbled, foamed and frothed
As flasks and undulating tubes were quaffed.

And who could doubt a curcubit
Sublimes magic elixirs fit,
To be the youth that humans sought
In this he strived and brooked for nought.
In labour and in oratory
He chased the quintessential he,
Which all served well his thoughts to hone
Who sought the all-elusive stone.

But had he sense to look within
The noble metal's plainly seen,
For Herme's wand, Caducceus
In language plain speaks out to us:
'If your quicksilver mind be stilled
Your deepest wishes are fulfilled'

As above, so below.

Sonnet 54

WILLIAM SHAKESPEARE (1564–1616)

O, how much more doth beauty beauteous seem
By that sweet ornament which truth doth give!
The rose looks fair, but fairer we it deem
For that sweet odour which doth in it live.
The canker-blooms have full as deep a dye
As the perfumed tincture of the roses,
Hang on such thorns and play as wantonly
When summer's breath their masked buds discloses:
But, for their virtue only is their show,
They live unwoo'd and unrespected fade,
Die to themselves. Sweet roses do not so;
Of their sweet deaths are sweetest odours made:
And so of you, beauteous and lovely youth,
When that shall fade, my verse distills your truth.

Coming To Kiss Her Lips

EDMUND SPENSER (1552–99)

Coming to kiss her lips (such grace I found)
Meseemed I smelt a garden of sweet flowers,
That dainty odours from them threw around
For damsels fit to deck their lovers' bowers.
Her lips did smell like unto gilly flowers,
Her ruddy cheeks like unto roses red,
Her snowy brows like budded belamours,
Her lovely eyes like pinks but newly spread;
Her goodly bosom like a strawberry bed.
Her neck like to a bunch of columbines,
Her breasts like lilies ere their leaves be shed,
Her nipples like young blossomed jessamines
Such fragrant flowers do give most odorous smell;
But her sweet odour did them all excel.

A Fragrante Prayer

THE GARDENER'S LABYRINTH (1577)
DIDYMUS MOUNTAIN (THOMAS HILL)

I wish unto you by daily prayer and fruition
of the heavenly paradise crayving of the
omnipotent and provident god, the guider of
that gorgeous garden that hee would
vouchsafe to grante unto you the sweete
savour of his chiefe fragrante floures, that is
his comfort to cleave faste unto you, his
mercy to keepe you and his grace to guyde
you now and evermore.

To the Most Fair and Lovely Mistress Anne Soame

ROBERT HERRICK (1591–1674)

To smell those odours that do rise
From out the wealthy spiceries
So smells the flower of blooming clove;
Or roses smother'd in the stove:
So smells the air of spiced wine;
Or essences of Jessamine:
So smells the breath above the hives
When well the work of honey thrives;
And all the busy factors come
Laden with wax and honey home,
So smell those neat and woven bowers,
All over-arch'd with orange flowers;
And almond blossoms that do mix
To make rich these aromaticks
So smell those bracelets and those bands
Of amber chaft between the hands,
When thus enkindled they transpire
A noble perfume from the fire ...

Whenas the meanest part of her,
Smells like the maiden pomander,
This sweet she smells of what can be
More lik'd by her, or lov'd by mee.

Upon Julia's Unlacing Herself

ROBERT HERRICK (1591–1674)

Tell, if thou cans't (and truly) whence doth come
This Camphire, Storax, Spikenard, Galbanum:
These *Musks* these *Ambers*, and those other smells
(Sweet as *the Vestrie of the Oracles*.)
Ile tell thee; while my Julia did unlace
Her silken bodies, but a breathing space:
The passive aire such odour then assum'd,
As when to *Jove* Great *Juno* goes perfum'd.
Whose pure-Immortal body doth transmit
A scent, that fills both Heaven and Earth with it.

Ask Me No More

THOMAS CAREW (1595–1639)

Ask me no more where Jove bestows,
When June is past, the fading rose;
For in your beauty's orient deep
These flowers as in their causes, sleep.

Ask me no more whither do stray
The golden atoms of the day;
For in pure love heaven did prepare
Those powders to enrich your hair.

Ask me no more whither doth haste
The nightingale, when May is past;
For in your sweet dividing throat
She winters and keeps warm her note.

Ask me no more where those stars' light
That downwards fall in dead of night;
For in your eyes they sit, and there
Fixed become as in their sphere.

Ask me no more if East or West
The Phoenix builds her spicy nest;
For unto you at last she flies,
And in your fragrant bosom dies.

From Rhodon and Iris

RALPH KNEVET (1600–71)

Nor in her weeds alone is she so nice,
But rich perfumes she buys at any price:
Storax and spikenard she burns in her chamber,
And daubs herself with civet, musk, and amber.
With limbicks, vials, pots, her closet's fill'd,
Full of strange liquors, by rare art distill'd.
She hath vermilion and antimony,
Cerusse and sublimated mercury;
Waters she hath to make her face to shine,
Confections eke to clarifie her skin;
Lipsalves, and clothes of pure scarlet dye,
She hath, which to her cheeks she doth apply;
Ointment, wherewith she pargets o'er her face,
And lustrifies her beauties' dying grace.
She waters from the Morphews doth compose,
And many other things as strange as those;
Some made of daffodils, and some of lees,
Of Scarwolfe some, and some of rinds of trees;
With centory, sour grapes, and tarragon,
She maketh many a strange lotion.
Her skin she can both supple and refine,
With juice of lemons and with turpentine;
The marrow of the hernshaw and the deer
She takes likewise, to make her skin look clear.

Sweet water she distills, which she composes
    Of flowers, or oranges, woodbine, or roses.
The virtues of jessimine or threeleaved grasse
    She doth imprison in a brittle glass:
With civit, muske, and odours far more rare,
    These liquors sweet incorporated are.
Lees she can make that turn a haire that's old,
    Or colour'd ill, into a hue of gold.
Of horses, bears, cats, camels, conies, snakes,
Whales, herons, bittourns, strange oils she makes;
With which dame Nature's errors she corrects,
    Using art's help to supply all defects.

A Nosegay for Laura

FRANCIS FAWKES (1720–77)

Come, ye fair ambrosial flowers,
Leave your beds and leave your bowers,
Blooming, beautiful and rare,
Form a posy for my Fair;
Fair and bright and blooming be,
Meet for such a nymph as she.

Let the young vermilion rose
A becoming blush disclose.
Such as Laura's cheeks display,
When she steals my heart away.

Add carnation's varied hue,
Moistened with the morning dew:
To the woodbine's fragrant join
Sprigs of snow white jessamine.

Add no more; already I
Shall alas! with envy die,
Thus to see my rival blessed
Sweetly dying on her breast.

Edict of George III, King of England

(1738–1820)

All women whether of rank or professional degree, whether virgins, maids or widows, that shall from after this Act impose upon, seduce and betray into matrimony any of his majesty's subjects by the use of scents, potions, cosmetics, washes, artificial teeth, false hair, Spanish wool, iron stays, hoops, high heels, shoes or bolstered hips, shall incur the penalty of the law now in force against witchcraft and like misdemenours, and that the marriage, upon conviction, shall stand null and void.

Cologne

SAMUEL TAYLOR COLERIDGE (1772–1834)

In Köhln, a town of monks and bones,
And pavements fanged with murderous stones
And rags and hags and hideous wenches;
I counted two and seventy stenches,
All well defined, and several stinks!
Ye Nymphs that reign o'er sewers and sinks,
The river Rhine, it is well known,
Doth wash your city of Cologne;
But tell me Nymphs, what power divine
Shall henceforth wash the river Rhine?

The Wallflower

WALTER SAVAGE LANDOR (1775–1864)

The place where soon I think to lie,
In its old creviced nook hard-by
Bears many a weed:
If parties bring you there, will you
Drop slily in a grain or two
Of wallflower seed?

I shall not see it, and (too sure!)
I shall not ever hear that your
Light step was there;
But the rich odour some fine day
Will, what I cannot do, repay
That little care.

From Ode to a Nightingale

JOHN KEATS (1795–1821)

I cannot see what flowers are at my feet,
Nor what soft incense hangs upon the boughs,
But in embalmed darkness, goes each sweet
Wherewith the seasonable month endows,
The grass, the thicket, and the fruit-tree wild;
White hawthorn, and the pastoral eglantine;
Fast-fading violets covered up in leaves;
And mid-May's eldest child,
The coming musk-rose, full of dewy wine,
The murmurous haunt of flies on summer leaves.

From The Sensitive Plant

PERCY BYSSHE SHELLEY (1792–1822)

The Snowdrop, and then the violet
Arose from the ground with warm rain wet,
And their breath was mixed with fresh odour, sent
From the turf, like the voice and the instrument.

Then the pied wind-flowers and the tulip tall,
And narcissi, the fairest among them all,
Who gaze on their eyes in the stream's recess,
Till they die of their own dear loveliness.

And the Naiad-like lily of the vale,
Whom youth makes so fair and passion so pale
That the light of its tremulous bells is seen
Through their pavilions of tender green;

And the hyacinth purple, and white, and blue,
Which flung from its bells a sweet peal anew
Of music so delicate and intense,
It was felt like an odour within the sense;

And the rose like a nymph to the bath addressed,
Which unveiled the depth of her glowing breast,
Till, fold after fold, to the fainting air
The soul of her beauty and love laid bare:

And the wand-like lily, which lifted up,
As a Maenad, its moonlight-coloured cup,
Till the fiery star, which is its eye,
Gazed through clear dew on the tender sky;

And the jessamine faint, and the sweet tuberose,
The sweetest flower for scent that blows;
And all rare blossoms from every clime
Grew in that garden in perfect prime.

Le Parfum

From UN FANTÔME, LES FLEURS DU MAL XXVIII
CHARLES BAUDELAIRE (1821–67)

Lecteur, as – tu quelquefois respiré
Avec ivresse et lente gourmandise
Ce grain d'encens qui remplit une église,
Ou d'un sachet le musc invétéré?

Charme profound, magique, dont nous grise
Dans le presént le passé restauré!
Ainsi l'amant sur un corps adoré
Du souvenir cueille la fleur exquise.

De ses cheveux élastiques et lourds
Vivant sachet, encensoir de l'alcôve,
Une senteur montait, sauvage et fauve,

Et des habits, mousseline ou velours,
Tout imprégnés de sa jeunesse pure,
Se dégageait un parfum de fourrure.

Awakenings

MARCEL PROUST (1871–1922)

Let a noise or a scent, once heard or once more smelt, be heard or smelt again, and immediately the permanent and habitually concealed essence of things is liberated and our true self which seemed to be dead but was not altogether dead, is awakened and reanimated.

Love and Sleep

ALGERNON CHARLES SWINBURNE (1837–1909)

Lying asleep between the strokes of night
I saw my love lean over my sad bed,
Pale as the duskiest lily's leaf or head,
Smooth-skinned and dark, with bare throat made to bite,
Too wan for blushing and too warm for white,
But perfect-coloured without white or red.
And her lips opened amorously, and said—
I wist not what, saving one word—Delight,
And all her face was honey to my mouth,
And all her body pasture to mine eyes;
The long lithe arms and hotter hands than fire,
The quivering flanks, hair smelling of the south,
The bright light feet, the splendid supple thighs
And glittering eyelids of my soul's desire.

Perfume

ARTHUR SYMONS (1865–1945)

Shake out your hair about me so,
That I may feel the stir and scent
Of those vague odours come and go
The way our kisses went.

Night gave this priceless hour of love,
But now the dawn steals in apace,
And amorously bends above
The wonder of your face.

'Farewell' between our kisses creeps,
You fade, a ghost, upon the air;
Yet, ah! The vacant place still keeps
The odour of your hair.

Memory

From 'LONDON NIGHTS' 1885
ARTHUR SYMONS (1865–1945)

As a perfume doth remain
In the folds where it hath lain,
So the thought of you, remaining
Deeply folded in my brain,
Will not leave me, all things leave me:
You remain.

Other thoughts may come and go,
Other moments I may know
That shall waft me in their going,
As a breath blown too and fro,
Fragrant memories, fragrant memories
Come and go.

Only thoughts of you remain
In my heart where they have lain,
Perfumed thoughts of you, remaining,
A hid sweetness, in my brain.
Others leave me; all things leave me:
You remain.

White Heliotrope

From 'LONDON NIGHTS'
ARTHUR SYMONS (1865–1945)

The feverish room and that white bed
The tumbled skirts upon the chair,
The novel flung half-open where
Hat, hair-pins puffs and paints are spread;

The mirror that has sucked your face
Into its secret deep of deeps,
And there mysteriously keeps
Forgotten memories of grace;

And you, half dressed, and half awake,
Your slant eyes strangely watching me,
And I who watch you drowsily,
With eyes that, having slept not, ache;

This (need one dread! Nay dare one hope!)
Will rise, a ghost of memory, if
Ever again my handkerchief
Is scented with white heliotrope.

Odour

THEODORE WRATISLAW (1871–1933)

So vague, so sweet a long regret!
So sweet, so vague a perfume
That lingers lest regret forget,
A memory from an old-world tomb
Where vainly sunshine gleams and vainly raindrops fret,
And dying summer's wind breath goes
So lightly over petals of the fallen rose.

Autumnal starlight, scents of hay
Beneath the full September moon,
And then, ah! Then! The sighing tune
That fades and yet is fain to stay:
Ah! Weep for pleasures dead too soon,
While like the love-song of an ancient day
The distant music of the perfume dies away.

Eros D'aute

THEODORE WRATISLAW (1871–1933)

Crimson nor yellow roses, nor
The savour of the mounting sea
Are worth the perfume I adore
That clings to thee.

The languid lilies tire,
The changeless waters weary me
I ache with passionate desire
Of thine and thee.

There are but these things in the world —
Thy mouth of fire,
Thy breasts, thy hands, thy hair uncurled
And my desire!

Hothouse Flowers

THEODORE WRATISLAW (1871–1933)

I hate the flower of wood or common field.
I cannot love the primrose nor regret
The death of any shrinking violet,
Nor even the cultured garden's banal yield.

The silver lips of lilies virginal,
The full deep bosom of the enchanted rose
Please less than flowers glass-hid from frost and snows
For whom an alien heat makes festival.

I love those flowers reared by man's careful art,
Of heady scents and colours: strong of heart
Or weak that die beneath the touch of knife,

Some rich as sin and some as virtue pale,
And some as subtly infamous and frail
As she whose love still eats my soul and life.

From The Picture of Dorian Gray

OSCAR WILDE (1854–1900)

And so he would now study perfumes and the secrets of their manufacture, distilling heavily scented oils and burning odourous gums from the East. He saw that there was no mood of the mind that had not its counterparts in the sensuous life, and set himself to discover their true relations, wondering what there was in Frankincense that made one mystical, and in Ambergris that stirred one's passions, and in Violets that woke the memory of dead romances, and in Musk that troubled the brain, and in Champac that stained the imagination; and seeking often to elaborate a real psychology of perfumes, and to estimate the several influences of sweet-smelling roots, and scented pollen-laden flowers, or aromatic balms, and of dark and fragrant woods; of spikenard, that sickens, of hovenia, that makes men mad, and of Aloes that are said to be able to expel melancholy for the soul.

A Lure

DAVID PYBUS (1947–)

Before I saw her, I sensed her...
Unwittingly entering the perfumed
Sphere of influence that
Her aura had flung out into dark space.

I crossed the event horizon of her being,
As my soul, joyfully,
And with complete abandon,
Entered her Universe.

She had spun
An aromatic web
Of enchantment
And I was won
And I was lost.

The Connoisseur of Woodsmoke

From THE SHINING LEVELS: THE STORY OF A MAN WHO
WENT BACK TO NATURE BY JOHN WYATT (1925–2006)

I soon became a connoisseur of woodsmoke. For fragrance, in my opinion, there is little to match Juniper; I would stack the wood aside against the days I had visitors. Apple and well-seasoned cherry are pure luxury too. Holly and birch have a clean tang. Ash, particularly green ash, smells like washing day. Old oak has an honest, pungent, lusty smell as you would expect. The other hardwoods are hardly worth a mention smoke-wise. The softwoods; pine, spruce or larch are rather vulgar; but there is something to be said for a really old vintage larch root. Once one gets the taste for smoking wood it is possible to mix and obtain subtle flavours; and invent recipes. Prepare a fire base of larch kindling; add well-seasoned oak until the logs redden deeply; place one large back log of holly, and add, from the fire back to the front, one crab-apple log, one well-dried cherry and one of birch. An ideal after-dinner mixture.

Ithaka

C. P. CAFAVY (1863–1933)

As you set out for Ithaka
hope your road is a long one,
full of adventure, full of discovery.
Laistrygonians, Cyclops,
angry Poseidon – don't be afraid of them:
you'll never find things like that on your way
as long as you keep your thoughts raised high,
as long as a rare excitement
stirs your spirit and your body.
Laistrygonians, Cyclops,
wild Poseidon – you won't encounter them
unless you bring them along inside your soul,
unless your soul sets them up in front of you.

Hope your road is a long one.
May there be many summer mornings when,
with what pleasure, what joy,
you enter harbours you're seeing there for the first time;
may you stop at Phoenician trading stations
to buy fine things,
mother of pearl and coral, amber and ebony,
sensual perfume of every kind –
as many sensual perfumes as you can;
and may you visit many Egyptian cities
to learn and go on learning from their scholars.

Keep Ithaka always in your mind.
Arriving there is what you're destined for.
But don't hurry the journey at all.
Better if it lasts for years,
so you're old by the time you reach the island,
wealthy with all you've gained on the way,
not expecting Ithaka to make you rich.

Ithaka gave you the marvellous journey.
Without her you wouldn't have set out.
She has nothing left to give you now.
And if you find her poor, Ithaka won't have fooled you.
Wise as you will have become, so full of experience,
you'll have understood by then what these Ithakas mean.

Sent

DAVID PYBUS (1947–)

When I sit and close my eyes,
Strange sensations can arise,
And my spirit 'cross the boundless ocean goes.
For my memory's strongly stirred,
And my senses gently whirred
By the recollective power of my nose.

Incense from a joss-stick's smoke,
Can sweet memories evoke,
Of a time and place that I hold dear to heart.
And I love to spend my time
In some fascinating clime
Half a world away from my own homely hearth.

Scents from precious flowers may
Bring me visions bright as day,
Of far places where my feet have often stood.
Perfumes drifting on the breeze
Take me back with seeming ease,
And I'd like to bring you with me if you would?

Off to Mexico we go,
When the smell is sweet aloe,
Bougainvillaea is the scent of Caribbee.
Fragrance mixed with spice and sand,
Gives the souks of Samarkand,
Grand Bazaars of Istanbul are there to see.

Eucalyptus takes us to Australia's shores,
Sensual jasmine to the mounts of the Azores,
Archipelagos I rove
Stirred by pungent smell of clove,
Catching all the fragrant odours far from home!

Then the perfumed hops of Kent,
Bring me back with their soft scent,
And I find myself in England once again,
Where cut-grass and red-rose bloom,
Gently drift into the room,
As I watch the drizzled mist and summer rain.

THE
AMERICAS

To Celia

BEN JONSON (1572–1637)

Drink to me only with thine eyes,
And I will pledge with mine;
Or leave a kiss but in the cup,
And I'll not look for wine.
The thirst, that from the soul doth rise,
Doth ask a drink divine;
But might I of Jove's nectar sup.
I would not change for thine.

I sent thee, late, a rosy wreath,
Not so much honouring thee,
As giving it a hope, that there
It could not withered be,
But thou thereon did'st only breathe,
And sent'st it back to me;
Since when it grows, and smells, I swear,
Not of itself; but thee.

From Bermudas

ANDREW MARVELL (1621–78)

Where the remote Bermudas ride,
In the ocean's bosom unespied,
From a small boat, that rowed along,
The listening winds received this song:

'What should we do but sing His praise
That led us through the watery maze,
Unto an isle so long unknown,
And yet far kinder than our own?

Where He the huge sea-monsters wracks,
That lift the deep upon their backs;
He lands us on a grassy stage,
Safe from the storms, and prelate's rage.

He gave us this eternal spring
Which here enamels everything,
And sends the fowls to us in care
On daily visits through the air.

He hangs in shades the orange bright
Like golden lamps in a green night,
And does in the pomegranates close
Jewels more rich than Ormus shows.

He makes the figs our mouths to meet,
And throws the melons at our feet;
But apples plants of such a price,
No tree could ever bear them twice.

With cedars chosen by His hand
From Lebanon He stores the land;
And makes the hollow seas that roar
Proclaim the ambergris on shore.

He cast (of which we rather boast)
The Gospel's pearl upon our coast;
And in these rocks for us did frame
A temple where to sound His name.

O! let our voice His praise exalt
Till it arrive at Heaven's vault,
When then (perhaps) rebounding may
Echo beyond the Mexique bay!'

Thus sung they in the English boat
An holy and a cheerful note;
An all the way to guide their chime,
With falling oars they kept the time.

Meditation 9

PHILIP PAIN (ca.1666)

Man's life is like a Rose, that in the Spring,
Begins to blossome, fragrant smells to bring:
Within a day or two, behold death's sent,
A publick messenger of discontent.
Lord grant, that when my Rose begins to fade,
I may behold an Everlasting shade.

From The song of Hiawatha

HENRY WADSWORTH LONGFELLOW (1807–82)

Looking still at Hiawatha,
Looking at fair Laughing Water,
Sang he softly, sang in this wise:
'Onaway! Awake! Beloved!
Thou the wild-flower of the forest!
Thou the wild-bird of the prairie!
Thou with eyes so soft and fawn-like!
If thou only lookest at me,
I am happy, I am happy,
As the lilies of the prairie,
When they feel the dew upon them!
Sweet thy breath is as the fragrance
Of the wild-flowers in the morning,
As their fragrance is at evening,
In the moon when leaves are falling.

To Helen

EDGAR ALLAN POE (1809–49)

Helen, thy beauty is to me
Like those Nicean barks of yore,
That gently o'er a perfumed sea,
The weary, way-worn wanderer bore
To his own native shore.

On desperate seas long wont to roam,
Thy hyacinth hair, thy classic face,
Thy Naiad airs have brought me home
To the glory that was Greece,
And the grandeur that was Rome.

Lo! In yon window-niche
How statue-like I see thee stand,
The agate lamp within thy hand!
Ah! Psyche, from the regions which
Are Holy land!

Smoke

HENRY DAVID THOREAU (1817–62)

Light-winged smoke, Icarian bird,
Melting thy passion in thy upward flight,
Lark without song, and messenger of dawn,
Circling above the hamlets as thy nest,
Or else, departing dream, and shadowy form
Of midnight vision, gathering up thy skirts;
By night star-veiling, and by day
Darkening the light and blotting out the sun;
Go thou my incense upward from this hearth,
And ask the gods to pardon this clear flame.

Ambergris

HERMAN MELVILLE (1819–91)

From MOBY DICK, CHAPTER 92

Now this ambergris is a very curious substance, and so important as an article of commerce, that in 1791 a certain Nantucket-born Captain Coffin was examined at the bar of the English House of Commons on that subject. For at that time, and indeed until comparatively late day, the precise origin of ambergris remained, like amber itself, a problem to the learned. Though the word ambergris is but the French compound for grey amber, yet the two substances are quite distinct. For amber, though at times found on the sea-coast, is also dug up in some far inland soils, whereas ambergris is never found except upon the sea. Besides, amber is a hard, transparent, brittle, odourless substance, used for mouth-pieces to pipes, for beads and ornaments, but ambergris is soft, waxy, and so highly fragrant and spicy that it is largely used in perfumery, in pastiles, precious candles, hair powders, and pomatum. The Turks use it in cooking, and also carry it to Mecca, for the same purpose that frankincense is carried to St. Peter's in Rome. Some wine merchants drop a few grains into claret, to flavour it. Who would think, then, that such fine ladies and gentlemen should regale themselves with an essence found in the inglorious bowels of a sick whale. Yet so it is. By some, ambergris is supposed to be the cause, and by others the effect, of the dyspepsia in the whale.

How to cure such dyspepsia it were hard to say, unless by administering three or four boat loads of Brandreth's pills, and then running out of harm's way, as labourers do in blasting rocks.

I have forgotten to say that there were found in this ambergris, certain hard, round, bony plates, which at first Stubb thought might be sailors' trouser buttons; but it afterwards turned out that they were nothing more than pieces of small squid bones embalmed in that manner. Now that the incorruption of this most fragrant ambergris should be found in the heart of such decay: is this nothing? Bethink thee of the saying of Saint Paul in Corinthians about corruption and incorruption: how that we are sown in dishonour, but raised in glory. And likewise call to mind that saying of Paracelsus about what it is that maketh the best musk. Also forget not the strange fact that of all things of ill-savour, Cologne-water in its rudimental manufacturing stages, is the worst.

Compiler's note:
The great value of ambergris, which is unique to the sperm whale, and used for the Coronation oil of the Kings and Queens of England, probably explains the fact that whales washed up on the coasts of the United Kingdom are legally Crown property.

From Waikiki

RUPERT BROOKE (1887–1915)

Warm perfumes like a breath from wine and tree
Drift down the darkness. Plangent, hidden from eyes,
Somewhere an eukaleli thrills and cries
And stabs with pain the night's brown savagery;
And dark scent's whisper; and dim waves creep to me,
Gleam like a woman's hair, stretch out, and rise;
And new stars burn into the ancient skies,
Over the murmurous soft Hawaian sea.

And I recall, lose, grasp, forget again,
And still remember, a tale I have heard, or known,
An empty tale of idleness and pain,
Of two that loved – or did not love – and one
Whose perplexed heart did evil, foolishly,
A long while since, and by some other sea.

The Flower-fed Buffaloes

VACHEL LINDSAY (1879–1931)

The flower-fed buffaloes of the spring
In the days of long ago,
Ranged where the locomotives sing
And the prairie flowers lie low.
The tossing, blooming, perfumed grass
Is swept away by the wheat,
Wheels and wheels and wheels spin by
In the spring that is still sweet.
But the flower-fed buffaloes of the spring
Left us, long ago.
They gore no more, they bellow no more,
They trundle around the hills no more.
With the Blackfeet, lying low
With the Pawnees lying low,
Lying low.

The Earth is Precious

ADAPTATION OF SUQUAMISH CHIEF
SEATHL'S SPEECH GIVEN IN 1854

The Great Chief in Washington sends word that he wishes to buy our land. The Great Chief also sends us words of friendship and goodwill. This is kind of him since we know he has little need of friendship in return. But we will consider your offer, for we know if we do not do so, the white man may come with guns and take our land.

What Chief Seathl says, the Great Chief in Washington can count on as truly as our White brothers can count on the return of the Seasons. My words are like the stars, they do not set.

How can you buy or sell the sky, the warmth of the land? The idea is strange to us. If we do not own the freshness of the air and the sparkle of the water, how can you buy them from us? We will decide in our time.

Every part of the earth is sacred to my people. Every shining pine needle, every sandy shore, every mist in the dark woods, every clearing and humming insect is holy to the memory and experience of my people. The sap which courses through the trees carries the memory and experience of the red man.

We know that the white man does not understand our ways. One portion of the land is the same to him as the next, for he is a stranger who comes in the night and takes from the land whatever he needs.

The earth is not his brother, but his enemy, and when he has conquered it, he moves on. He leaves his fathers' graves behind, and he does not care. He kidnaps the earth from his children, he does not care. His fathers' graves and his children's birthright are forgotten.

He treats his mother, the earth, and his brother, the sky, as things to be bought, plundered, sold like sheep or bright beads. His appetite will devour the earth and leave only a desert.

The white man's dead forget about the country of their birth when they go to walk among the stars. Our dead never forget this beautiful earth, for it is the mother of the red man. We are part of the earth, and it is part of us. The perfumed flowers are our sisters, the deer, the horse, the great eagle, these are our brothers.

What is man without the beasts? If all the beasts were gone, men would die from a great loneliness of spirit, for whatever happens to the beasts soon happens to the man. All things are connected.

Teach your children what we have taught our children – the earth is our mother. Whatever befalls the earth befalls the sons of the earth. If men spit upon the ground, they spit upon themselves.

This we know. The earth does not belong to man,

man belongs to the earth. This we know: all things are connected, like the blood which unites one family. All things are connected.

Man does not weave the web of life. He is merely a strand in it. Whatever he does to the web he does to himself.

There is no quiet place in the white man's city, no place to hear the leaves of spring or the rustle of insect's wings; but because I am a savage and do not understand the clatter only seems to insult the ears, and what is there to life if a man cannot hear the cry of the lovely whippoorwhill or the argument of the frogs around a pool at night.

The Indian prefers the soft sound of the wind, darting over the face of the pond, and the smell of the wind itself, cleansed by a midday rain or scented with pinon pine: the air is precious to the red man.

For all things share the same breath: the beast, the trees, the man. The White man does not seem to notice the air he breathes. Like a man dying, for many days he is numb to the smell of his own stench.

When the last Red Man has vanished from the earth, and the memory is only in the shadow of a cloud, moving across the prairie, these shores and these forests will still hold the spirit of my people, for they love the earth as the newborn loves his mother's heartbeat.

If we sell you our land, love it as we have loved it, care for it as we have cared for it. Hold in your mind the memory of the land, as it is when you take it, and with all your strength and with all your might and with all your heart, preserve it for your children and love it as God loves us all.

And if we sell you our land, you must keep it apart and sacred, as a place where even the white man can go to taste the wind that is sweetened by the meadow's flowers.

One thing we know, our God is the same God. The earth is precious to Him. Even the white man cannot be exempt from a common destiny. We may be brothers after all. We shall see.

Roots and Leaves

From LEAVES OF GRASS (CALAMUS)
WALT WHITMAN (1819–92)

Roots and leaves themselves alone are these,
Scents brought to men and women
From the wild woods and pond-side,
Breast-sorrel and pinks of love,
Fingers that wind around tighter than vines,
Gushes from the throats of birds,
Hid in the foliage of trees as the sun is risen;
Breezes of land and love set from living shores
To you on the living sea –
To you O sailors!
Frost-mellow'd berries and Third month twigs,
Offer'd fresh to young persons wandering out in the fields
When the winter breaks up.
Lover buds put before you and within you,
Whoever you are.
Buds to be unfolded on the old terms;
If you bring the warmth of the sun to them,
they will open and bring form, color, perfume, to you;
If you become the aliment and the wet
They will bear flowers, fruits, tall branches and trees.

The Sign

AMADO NERVO (1870–1919)

Talk not to all about things sublime and essential.
Seek the level of the person with whom you speak.
So as not to humble and distress them.

Be frivolous too when you are with the frivolous,
But once in a while, as if unsought, or even as
thoughtlessly,
Drop into their cup on the foam of frivolity,
A very small petal from the flower of your dreams.

If it is not noticed, recover it courteously,
And, always smiling, go on your way.
If, however, someone picks up the frail, small petal
And examines it, inhales its fragrance,
Give them forthwith and carefully a sign of discreet
understanding.

Let them behold one or a few of the marvellous flowers of
your garden,
Tell them of the invisible Divinity which surrounds us
all,
The open sesame of true Freedom.

EPILOGUE

Earth Scent

DAVID PYBUS

I've often thought
As we spin through space
If planet earth
Leaves a scented trace?

Some smell to fill the vacuum there,
A clue for aliens that we're here
Some molecules of Chanel 5®
Might indicate we're all alive?

Or coffee brewing on the stove,
Now there's a pleasant thought by Jove!
A whiff of bread, fresh on the rise,
Or bacon butties on the braais.

And vinegar on fish and chips,
Aromas that will lick their lips,
Or aromatic curry sauce
With extra puppadums of course!

The meaty mix of a Big Mac
Might make them turn their spaceship back
Or heady Rastafarian mash
Of baccy-smoke with added hash.

Or rainfall on a summer's day
Mingled well with thickened clay
Or incense from a billion prayers
Could make ET reverse the gears.

But he won't come for cars I know
Which spew exhaust fumes of C.O.
And, God forbid, what makes him go
Could be the smell of our B.O.!

Glossary

Alabaster	A dense, fine-grained gypsum, often white and translucent, that is often carved for ornaments and figurines
Alembic	Alchemical apparatus used in distillation
Aloes	Strong-smelling plant of genus aloe
Aludel	Alchemical apparatus
Amber	Fossilised tree-resin
Ambergris	Natural product of sperm whale composed of bones and other debris which is spewed onto the surface of the sea, and develops a marvellous aroma. Used as a fixative in perfumes
Ambrosia	Food of the gods
Aphrodite	Greek Goddess of Love
Aphrodisiac	Love stimulant, arousing or intensifying sexual desire
Athanor	Alchemical apparatus-furnace
B.O.	Body odour
Bain-Marie	Alchemical apparatus – water bath
Balm	A soothing, healing ointment, often fragrant
Belamour	Lovers, or suitors
Benzoin	Aromatic tree-resin found mainly in Thailand. Used in perfumery
Bergamot	Essential citrus oil from bitter orange tree, used in perfumery, particularly Eau de Colognes
Betel	Leaves of Piper betle. Chewed as a mild stimulant, it gives a bright red colour to teeth and gums
Bittournes	Bitterns. A species of wading bird

Braais	Barbecues in South Africa
C.O.	Carbon Monoxide
Calamus	A wild iris known as the sweet flag, or its aromatic root
Camphire	Camphor
Canker-blooms	Flowers
Cassia	A variety of cinnamon
Censer	Special vessel for burning incense
Centory	Century Plant. The Aloe Plant
Cerusse	Cosmetic containing white lead
Cetewale	Aromatic root, such as Galangal or Valerian
Chypre	French for Cyprus
Cinnabar	A reddish mineral that is the main ore of mercury and is sometimes used as a pigment; mercuric sulphide
Cinnamon	A spice made from the inner bark of any of several tropical Asian trees
Civet (also Civit)	Abyssinian (Ethiopian) wild cat. In the last century was farmed for Civet, a territorial marker scent used as a fixative in perfumery
Columbines	Flower with beak-like (dove) spurs
Copra	Dried coconut flesh, from which oil is removed for use in various products
Curcubit	Alchemical instrument used in sublimation
Cuttlefish	Any of several molluscs with calcified internal shells and ten tentacles attached to the head
Cyclops	One-eyed giant of Greek myth
Cyprian	Native of Cyprus
Djinni	Alternative spelling of Genie
Ephemeral	Lasting for only a short period
Eukaleli	Alternative spelling of Ukelele. Hawaiian stringed instrument
Factors	Bees
Frankincense	Incense favoured by the French (Frank) knights and used in Christian ceremonies
Galbanum	Aromatic root grown mainly in Iran. Has been used in perfume and incense for thousands of years, and gives off a 'green' aroma

Gilly flowers	Clove pink (Dianthus Caryophyllus)
Icarian	From Icarus, of Greek legend, who attempted to fly with feathers gummed by wax
Ithaka	Island home of Ulysses (Odysseus). His ten-year voyage home from the siege of Troy was the subject of Homer's *Odyssey*
Jessamines	Jasmin
Joss stick	Incense stick
Jove	The Roman god Jupiter
Ka	Soul
Kimono	A long, loose-fitting Japanese robe having wide sleeves and a broad sash
Koh	Incense (Japanese). Also aloeswood, a special wood prized in the making of fine incense (not to be confused with aloes)
Kubla (Kublai) Khan	Mongol emperor of China. Grandson of Genghis
Ladanon	Labdanum
Labdanum	A sticky, resinous material from the Cistus Labdanum, or Rock Rose, found throughout the Mediterranean region, but mainly in Crete and Cyprus
Laistrogonians	Cannibal giants of Greek myth
Limbicks	Alembics (q.v.)
Malabar	Region on West coast of India
Maturine	Mature
Medle	Mix
Mikan	Asian Fruit
Musk	Territorial marker scent from musk deer used in the last century as a fixative and ingredient for perfume. The deer is native only to China, Tibet and Nepal
Musmee	Japanese woman
Myrrh	A sweet-smelling gum exuded by several related trees and shrubs native to India, Arabia and East Africa, and used in perfume and incense

Nard	Spikenard (q.v.)
Nirvana	A state of harmony, bliss, peace, or joy
Obi	A wide sash worn at the waist over a Japanese kimono
Omogi	Article of Japanese clothing
Onycha	Operculum (valve closing mouth of shell) of a sea snail
Oratory	A small chapel or room for private worship or prayer
Ordinall	Order or ranking
Parget	Plaster
Pelikan	Alchemical apparatus
Plangent	Having a sad or mournful sound; plaintive
Poseidon	Greek God of the sea (Roman Neptune)
Puffers	A derogatory name for alchemists
Quintessential	A concentrated and purified form of something
Quicksilver	Mercury (mercurial)
Rancou	Amerindian red body paint
Soote	Sweet
Spikenard	A precious herb found in the foothills of the Himalayas. The root is used to obtain an essential oil for perfumery, and is thought in Indian folklore to be an Aphrodisiac. Features in the Bible
Stacte	Form of Myrrh – highest quality
Storax	An aromatic resin used in perfumery
Vermilion	A bright red pigment made of mercuric sulphide
Xanadu	Capital City of the Mongol Emperor Kublai Khan in China

Bibliography

Allen, Charles	Tales from the South China Seas	Futura 1982
Baudelaire, Charles	Les Fleurs du Mal	Classique Larrouse 1993
C. P. Cafavy	Collected Poems	Chatto 1998
Conrad, Joseph	Lord Jim	Penguin Classics 1998
Ellman	New Oxford Book of American verse	Oxford University Press
Fischer-Rizzi, Suzanne	The Complete Incense Book	Sterling 1996
Fitzgerald, Edward	Rubaiyat of Omar Khayyam	Dover Publications 1990
Geddes, Gerda	Looking for the Golden Needle	Manna Media 1991
Genders, Roy	A History of Scent	Hamilton 1972
Golden, Arthur	Memoirs of a Geisha	Random Books 2001
Groom, Nigel	The Perfume Book	Chapman & Hall 1992
Heredotus	The Histories	Penguin Classics 1996
Holdsworth, R. V.	Arthur Symons – Poetry and Prose	Carcanet Books 1990
Holmes, Robin	A Country Calendar of Rural Verse	Methuen 1980
Kennett, Francis	A History of Perfume	Maynard 1975
Kirkup, James	Shepherding Winds	Blackie 1969
Melville, Herman	Moby Dick	Penguin Classics 1998
Pybus, David	Kodo, The Way of Incense	Tuttle 2001
Whitfield, Susan	Life along the Silk Road	John Murray 1999
Holy Bible	King James Edition	
The Nation's favourite poems		BBC Publications 1999

Founded 1674

The crest of the William Harvey Grammar School above
is modelled on the crest of a descendant of Sir William
Harvey who fought at Trafalgar and was in command
of the three ships named – *Temeraire, Redoubtable* and *Fougeux*.
We are grateful to the Harvey Grammar School, Folkestone,
Kent, for permission to reproduce the crest.